W9-CRY-950

Reptile World
Chameleons

by Cari Meister

Bullfrog
Books

Ideas for Parents and Teachers

Bullfrog Books let children practice reading informational text at the earliest reading levels. Repetition, familiar words, and photo labels support early readers.

Before Reading

- Discuss the cover photo. What does it tell them?

- Look at the picture glossary together. Read and discuss the words.

Read the Book

- "Walk" through the book and look at the photos. Let the child ask questions. Point out the photo labels.

- Read the book to the child, or have him or her read independently.

After Reading

- Prompt the child to think more. Ask: Have you ever seen a chameleon? Did it change color?

Bullfrog Books are published by Jump!
5357 Penn Avenue South
Minneapolis, MN 55419
www.jumplibrary.com

Library of Congress Cataloging-in-Publication Data

Meister, Cari, author.
 Chameleons / by Cari Meister.
    Pages cm. — (Bullfrog books. Reptile world)
Summary: "This photo-illustrated book for beginning readers describes the physical features and behaviors of chameleons. Includes picture glossary and index."—Provided by publisher.
 Audience: Ages 5–8.
 Audience: K to grade 3.
 Includes index.
 ISBN 978-1-62031-194-3 (hardcover: alk. paper) —
 ISBN 978-1-62496-281-3 (ebook)
 1. Chameleons—Juvenile literature. I. Title.
 QL666.L23M45 2016
 597.95'6—dc23
                                              2014042728

Editor: Jenny Fretland VanVoorst
Series Designer: Ellen Huber
Book Designer: Michelle Sonnek
Photo Researcher: Michelle Sonnek

Photo Credits: All photos by Shutterstock except: age fotostock, 12–13; Alamy, 15; Corbis, 18–19; Getty, 6–7, 10–11, 20–21, 23tl, 23tr; iStock, 16–17, 24; Science Source Images, 8; Thinkstock, cover.

Printed in the United States of America at Corporate Graphics in North Mankato, Minnesota.

For my nephew, Parker—Auntie Mimi

Table of Contents

A Colorful Lizard

What is in the tree?

It is a chameleon.

Chameleons can change colors.

A chameleon
wants to hide.

He turns green.

Green helps him
blend in.

He looks for a mate.

He turns blue.

Bright colors will attract a mate.

It is cold.

This one turns brown.

Dark skin absorbs
more sunlight.

This chameleon
is hungry.

She sees a bug.

The bug moves.

Her eyes move.
They follow the bug.

15

She runs.
She is fast!
Where did her food go?

17

There it is!

She pushes out
her tongue.

It is long.

It is sticky.

tongue

She gets the bug.
Yum!

Parts of a Chameleon

eye
A chameleon can see very well; each eye can move separately.

tongue
A chameleon has a long, sticky tongue that can grab food fast.

feet
A chameleon's feet are very good at gripping branches.

tail
A chameleon has a very long tail that helps with balance; it can also be coiled up.

Picture Glossary

absorb
To take in and trap; dark skin can take in more sunlight than light skin.

blend in
To look like what is around you.

attract
To create interest; chameleons change color to attract a mate.

mate
An animal's partner; a chameleon needs a mate to make babies.

Index

To Learn More

Learning more is as easy as 1, 2, 3.

1) Go to www.factsurfer.com

2) Enter "chameleons" into the search box.

3) Click the "Surf" button to see a list of websites.

With factsurfer.com, finding more information is just a click away.